The Boy, the River, and the Fish Named Zed

NADINE JUDITH LYNCH, Ph.D.

iUniverse®

THE BOY, THE RIVER, AND THE FISH NAMED ZED

iUniverse books may be ordered through booksellers or by contacting:

iUniverse
1663 Liberty Drive
Bloomington, IN 47403
www.iuniverse.com
1-800-Authors (1-800-288-4677)

ISBN: 978-1-5320-0200-7 (sc)
ISBN: 978-1-5320-0201-4 (e)

Library of Congress Control Number: 2016911005

Print information available on the last page.

iUniverse rev. date: 07/07/2016

This beautiful book
belongs to:

_____

Once
upon a time...

Notes

In that small peaceful town in the midst of unpopularity,

where young and old alike go to get away from the hustle and bustle, occasionally.

Notes

Notes

He often went on summer
vacations with his family and
friends,
he would go down to the big tree
where the riverbank bends.

Running, and jumping, and playing
all day. Climbing the tree,
and pretending to be the acrobat
he saw on TV.

Notes

Notes

Hanging upside-down on that big, old, tree.
The one near the river, the quiet river that down the road eventually turns into a sea.

Quiet, and big, and proud it need not make a noise, not even a little sound.
With its many, many secrets and you know it will never tell.

Notes

Notes

That river spanning long and wide, with one little fish just doodling inside.

How great it is to be here and see the silent river that runs so deep, said the boy gleefully.

Notes

Notes

He always plays here where the cows once fed
and the children would lie down to rest their tired sleepy heads.

A little fish in a big river. Diving, and flipping, and disturbing the river's rest,
the little fish had only the river for a friend that was the best.

Notes

The boy on the hill who came down everyday
to climb the tree and roll in the hay,
would sit by the river and watch the fish play.

It would swim all day and do what fish do,
with no enemies to escape from and no friends to swim to.

Notes

Notes

When Winter came the river was a bit icy,
he wondered where the fish had gone, he hoped it didn't leave to go exploring in the sea.

Notes

Notes

Then he saw it on the other side
just floating away with the river
under its head,
it was just laying there as if the
river were its bed,
after a while to himself the boy said,
"My friend the fish, oh no he's
dead."

Notes

Did the river do this to him with
its silence running deep,
by not speaking to the fish and
not keeping him company?
Or did the little fish want to
die and just gave up instead?
Did it swim backward instead of
swimming ahead?
Did it make up its mind that it
wanted to be dead?

Notes

Notes

The boy could not believe that
the little fish was dead,
so he closed his eyes and opened
them again,
he expected to see him flipping,
and diving, and looking well fed,
but all he saw was his little fish
friend lodged on the riverbank,
oh Zed.

Notes

He turned and started walking
up the hill, hoping and wishing in
the back of his head
that the lonely little fish was
not really dead.
Then he stopped, and turned,
and looked at the other side of
the riverbank near the bend
and saw his friend the fish,
whom he named Zed.
And the fish was still dead!

Notes